Father Animals

by Kris Bonnell

A blackbird is a good father.
He feeds his hungry chicks.

3

A lion can be a good father.
He keeps his cubs safe.

A father penguin keeps
his chick safe and warm.
A penguin is a good father.

A fox can be a good father.
He plays with his kits.

10

A mother seahorse
gives her eggs
to a father seahorse.
He keeps the eggs safe.

Soon, the father seahorse has baby seahorses.
A seahorse is a very good father!